Manifest That Sh*t

A Journal for Ditching Self-Doubt and Actualizing Your Dreams

MONICA SWEENEY

CASTLE POINT BOOKS
NEW YORK

www.castlepointbooks.com

The Castle Point Books trademark is owned by Castle Point Publishing, LLC.
Castle Point books are published and distributed by St. Martin's Publishing Group.

ISBN 978-1-250-28520-1 (trade paperback)

Cover and interior design by Melissa Gerber
Images used under license by Shutterstock.com

Our books may be purchased in bulk for promotional, educational,
or business use. Please contact your local bookseller or the Macmillan
Corporate and Premium Sales Department at 1-800-221-7945,
extension 5442, or by email at MacmillanSpecialMarkets@macmillan.com.

First Edition: 2022

10 9 8 7 6 5 4 3 2 1

This Book Belongs To:

Sabrina

Manifest that shit!

Just kidding, magic isn't real. Or at least not the instant, wake-up-in-a-glorious-castle-with-great-fucking-hair kind of magic. The magic of manifesting involves concentrating on a wish or goal and being open to the interpretation that unveils itself to you. Putting your best foot forward, releasing *good energy* into the world, and opening your mind to possibilities have *very* real results. Manifesting is about synchronicity, *believing in yourself*, positive self-talk, and taking advantage of the sparkling gems that the world has laid out in front of you to lead you on the right path.

But what about that time the world fell apart and everything burst into flames? Yes, sometimes life smacks you in the face and it breaks your fucking heart. It can be

needlessly cruel or mercilessly dick-ish. But let's be clear: You did not manifest *that* shit. What you can manifest is how you heal, how you help others, and how you move on. Okay, but what if I can't help but stay pissed about something and end up in a never-ending loop of manifested badness? Totally possible! <u>Negative energy is its own power,</u> so here's your opportunity to cast it the hell out.

By sprinkling moments big and small with that good old *hell, yes* attitude, you'll be surprised by all the worthwhile things that are waiting for you. In this guided journal of peppy profanity, you'll find encouragement, inspiration, and a hefty dose of sass that will bring you exactly what you need to fend off the self-doubt that's holding you back, and to swing the door to new opportunities way the fuck open.

Speak to it AS THOUGH IT'S ALREADY happened.

—JENNIFER ANISTON,
THE DREW BARRYMORE SHOW

My Wish is My Command

Success—whether that comes in the form of a job, a new adventure, or figuring out that five-letter word puzzle without throwing your phone—is an attitude. Speak to your goals as if you have already achieved them, as if you already run that shit. What will you say to them?

I feel Happy. I Have money in the bank. My father is healthy. I have my own family. My husband loves me, like I love Him. I don't have to worry about my father and my retirment because I had made ~~onouth~~ a lot of money. ~~on my business.~~ ~~I have a marketing business.~~ ~~I manifest I will~~ ~~going to have a marketing business why has core and~~ ~~has as been my monifestion become truth.~~ I work with people, I have a team of people that Help me.

REBECCA: Do you believe in ghosts, Ted?

TED: I do, but more importantly, I think they need to believe in themselves.

—*TED LASSO*

Believe

It's all fun and games until you're feeling fucking invisible. When all you can do is be haunted by your own self-doubt, find the light in the darkness. What do you believe in about yourself? How do you want others to believe in you?

I beleve I can do It. I dont core If other don4 beleeve and me. I have my own self to do everything I want to get In Life. I am orgonized and I arcnive everytny I focus on. I beleve I can find love in myself and I can be happy on my own. I beleve I can Have a family and a Husband. I believe I can have disipline and arcnive olot of things.

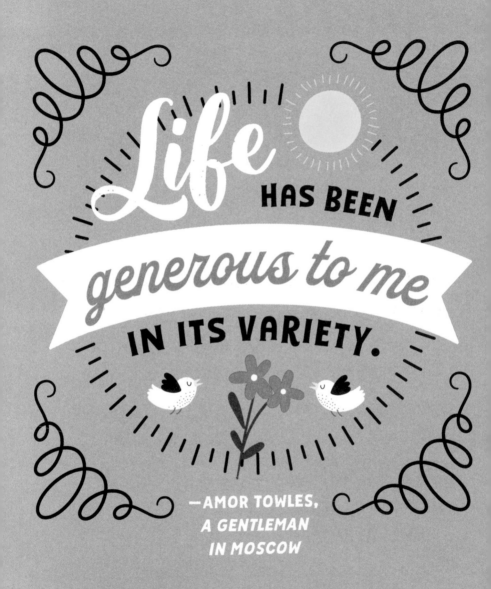

Life HAS BEEN generous to me IN ITS VARIETY.

—AMOR TOWLES,
A GENTLEMAN
IN MOSCOW

Level 3 Fun

Level 1 is actual fun! Level 2 is fun lite. Level 3 is decidedly not fun—it's the detour, the arduous trek, the most embarrassing shit of your entire life—but lessons are had and laughs come much, much later. Think of a Level 3 situation and what it means to you. How did a moment that seemed pretty shitty ultimately yield something greater?

① working not ② moving at to efferent homes. Helping my father to helping me, and ③ ~~but so easy at the beginning~~. to find peace!!!
finding a home and a job at a Cirques.

Shitty	Happness !!!
① working at.	Gain self steem (not easy in the beginning)
② Breaking out.	Finding peace.
③ moving out to the crques.	Getting to know myself
④ Having no Home	Having a Motor Home.
⑤ My father operation	expending time with them.
⑥ mrenzel ex.	having a great Relashnshp.
⑦ learning english	be able to undastand english

All's Fair in Love and Manifesting

Let's get scripting! What do you want in a partner or a romance? Repeat this line below to make it so (and also, you know, don't fucking settle).

I want a good person, a christen person.

I want ~~respect~~ mutual.

I want good communication.

~~No lies, no cheating.~~

He love me, I love him.

We love to spend time together.

We miss eachother

YOU CAN'T CHANGE
WHO YOU'VE BEEN.

It's never too late TO choose who you want TO become.

IDENTITY IS A DECISION,
NOT A DESTINY.

—ADAM GRANT

Voila!

Ever worry you were an asshole?
Real assholes don't worry about that.
If you've made mistakes in the past or felt
misunderstood in a way that nags at you,
what could you do differently next time?
What does your future ID look like?

Resentment Bringing my pass to my
Present when he was drinking. to Forgive.

- Overreacting to the lies and lies. to Breath.

- Not working on myself. execration -

- Not finishing anything -

- Being in toxic Relationship.

Independent
Smart
capoble.

Distance makes the **HEART GROW FONDER,** AND proximity makes the heart want to barf.

—MR. KULKARNI,
NEVER HAVE I EVER

Monet Status

Big dreams sure look pretty when you're looking at them from far away. Up close, those details can get muddy and messy and a little nauseating. What is it about the finer details or the closeness of something that turns you off or scares you? What's one thing that can help you make sense of it?

The amount of time spend doing something I don't have motivation. I wish I had some kind of feeling to be able the work it takes to do it.

Let's begin by TAKING A SMALLISH nap or two.

—A. A. MILNE,
WINNIE THE POOH

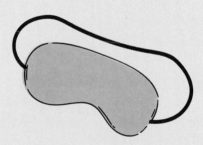

Give It a Fucking Rest

Zzzzzz...

Be kind to yourself! Take breaks when you need them. Your priorities will still be there when you wake up, so you may as well catch some Zs. What gets in the way of your relaxation? What's your ideal way to unwind?

Taking 5 min Break doing whatever is enough for me to take a rest and unwind my brain and feel like going back to my work.

Sleep.

tv.

createy

sex.

working out.

Going for a walk.

SELF LOVE

You can be a MILLIONAIRE... First, GET A MILLION DOLLARS.

—STEVE MARTIN,
COMEDY IS NOT PRETTY

Easy Peasy

A fun way to encourage someone is to make their idea feel unachievable! Just kidding. When has it felt like the barrier to entry for something you wanted was too high? When have you felt surprised that it came your way, or what messages can you send to yourself to keep the possibilities open?

Wake up and go sleep thinking that It working every day toward my goal. Keeping record of my improvements.

GET COMFORTABLE WITH *the*... IDEA THAT YOU WON'T KNOW WHAT'S GOOD UNTIL IT'S ALREADY HAPPENED.

—JAD ABUMRAD

Did You Miss the Manifest?!

Who knows! It's not always clear when good things are right in front of us, or when serendipity is jumping into action. Think back on parts of your past. What unexpected positives emerged when you weren't paying attention?

When I pray and I an specfic on what I want things happen and even If I don't want to make expeetation and. Think the is tne pason I ask god For. He is there and He show me everyday He is redlly what god send me.

DELUSIONS OF *grandeur*

MAKE ME FEEL A LOT BETTER ABOUT MYSELF.

—LILY TOMLIN

Beautiful Delusions

THIS IS YOUR FUTURE

Impossible is a concept you don't actually have to accept. What's something that other people think is impossible but you're convinced could be yours? What's one step toward it that would feel fucking great?

Making money on Youtube.
Having a family of my own.
Traveling around the world.
Living in a Mansion
Having financial Independence.
Getting of out of the Rat Race.
Helping my family.
See my self and family Healthy.

I don't want a *comparison* **hangover**

IT'S USELESS AND IT'S A WASTE OF

fucking time.

—KRISTEN BELL,
ARMCHAIR EXPERT

Contentment
Curious

Binging on tall pours of other people's happiness? Maybe don't! Comparison is exponential and it will leave you with all the aches and pains. The person you're comparing yourself to is doing the same with whatever the hell it is they're insecure about. Focus instead on what's in front of you. What brings you contentment?

Having money on my bank.

Be able to buy things I need. Food/water, etc...

helping others.

Working out.

Growing

Having a place to live comfortably.

Learning better English.

Having a good men with me.

There's a point where you go

WITH WHAT YOU'VE GOT.

Or you don't go.

—JOAN DIDION

Throw Shit at the Wall

Whenever you're feeling ill-equipped, keep this sage wisdom in mind: No one knows what the fuck they are doing. (Unless they are responsible for human lives or connecting internet routers.) Just start now! When did you dive headfirst into something without knowing what you were doing? What were the pros and cons of leaping blindly?

You can try new things, learn and gain experience.

You can always make mistakes.

You never stop trying and learning

You get to know yourself

You grow and expand yourself.

THERE'S
NO ROOM
 demons
WHEN
YOU'RE SELF-
POSSESSED.

—CARRIE FISHER

Demons, Be Damned

Cast out those big bads. What demons are getting in your way? If you could embody all the strength and power (And scary teeth? And maybe some slime?) that would send those other demons running, how would you do it?

Repeat MySelf I can do It.
I am Smart.
be Pacience. don't Quit.
Keep trying. Get some Rest. think.
Pray. Listen to GOD.

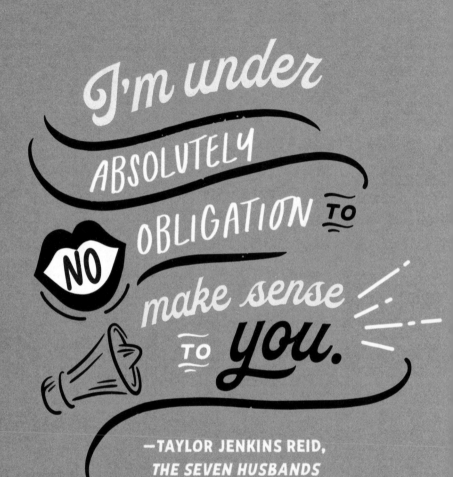

I'm under ABSOLUTELY NO OBLIGATION TO make sense TO you.

—TAYLOR JENKINS REID,
*THE SEVEN HUSBANDS
OF EVELYN HUGO*

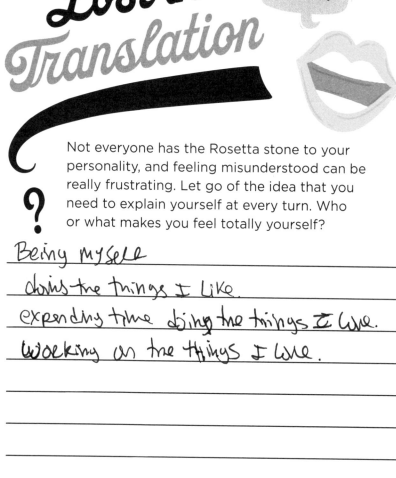

Lost in Translation

Huh?

Not everyone has the Rosetta stone to your personality, and feeling misunderstood can be really frustrating. Let go of the idea that you need to explain yourself at every turn. Who or what makes you feel totally yourself?

Being myself

doing the things I like.

expending time doing the things I love.

Working on the things I love.

WHEN FEAR GRIPS THE SOUL, *it's amazing* WHAT ONE CAN ACHIEVE.

—STANLEY TUCCI, TASTE

Hold On Tight

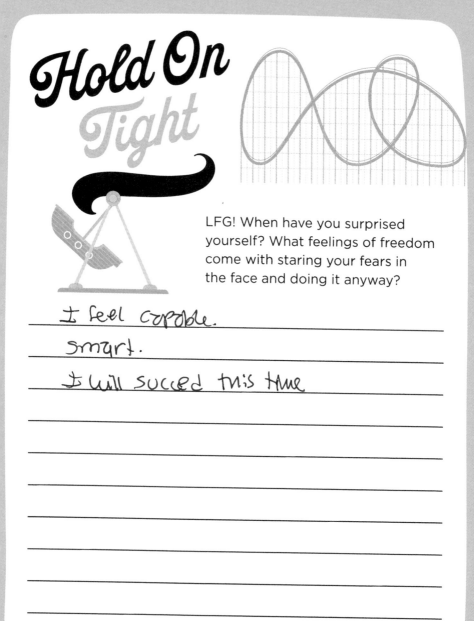

LFG! When have you surprised yourself? What feelings of freedom come with staring your fears in the face and doing it anyway?

I feel capable.

smart.

I will succed this time

THIS WAS JUST A BIG WASTE OF *time* AND FROWN LINES.

—DAVID ROSE,
SCHITT'S CREEK

Sad Face

Let's get one thing straight: Your feelings are valid. You should feel them and try to understand them. But like that avocado sitting on your counter or the resting rage face, there is such a thing as too much time. When have you been in a situation that you knew felt wrong but you slogged through it just to see if it would improve? What would feel good about identifying what's wrong for you and cutting it short?

leaving for ever

Going for a walk

Getting some Rest.

talking to God to find a solution.

All you have to do is to pay attention; LESSONS ALWAYS ARRIVE WHEN YOU ARE READY, AND IF YOU CAN READ THE SIGNS, YOU WILL LEARN *everything you need to know in order to take the next step.*

—PAULO COELHO, THE ZAHIR

Neon Signs

STOP

What signs speak to you? When have you felt like someone or something in the universe was trying to get your attention?

GOD is always trying to set my attention.

DON'T MAKE ME

· ME ·

AN

OPTIMIST.

YOU WILL RUIN MY

» Life «

—FLEABAG

Think Kinda Positively!

Take your salt with a grain of optimism. What kinds of negative predictions have you made so often that they feel like they come true? What specks of optimism could you sprinkle that could be yours instead?

I will be a black sheep master. and make millions.

If I could **BELIEVE** *in myself, why* **NOT GIVE OTHER** *improbabilities* **THE BENEFIT** *of the doubt?*

—DAVID SEDARIS,
HOLIDAYS ON ICE

Waltz into the Improbable

However you arrive at confidence—be it a hard-won conversation with yourself or a natural wellspring of gushing self-assuredness—don't be afraid to harness its power when it's there. When have you shown confidence in someone or something else and it gave them an edge? How does it feel to let other people surprise you?

not sure.

_____

_____

_____

_____

_____

_____

_____

_____

_____

I *Pretended* TO *be*

SOMEBODY I
WANTED TO BE

and I finally became that person. Or he became me. Or we met *at some point.*

—CARY GRANT

Nice to Meet You!

Don't be fake, just get into the character you want to be forever and ever. It's called ~~acting~~ manifesting. When those feelings of self-doubt come up—that you're not right for the role you're in, that you don't feel great in your own skin—muster up the confidence you think <u>you'd feel after achieving what you want</u>. Wield it now. What would that feel like?

RELETIve
Peace.
Confident.
Smart.

Every day

YOU HAVE TO
CHOOSE TO FIND
AND CULTIVATE YOUR OWN

Happiness.

—REESE WITHERSPOON

Let the Good Shit Spring Forth

Happiness is its own garden. It has seasons. It blossoms like nobody's watching. It wilts and occasionally gets infested with invasive species. But it will pop up again. Plant this garden on the page. What's in it?

learn every day trading

write my Journal feelings.

learn english.

Get things done. Calls. etc...

Cook. and eat Healthy

Keep moving your body.

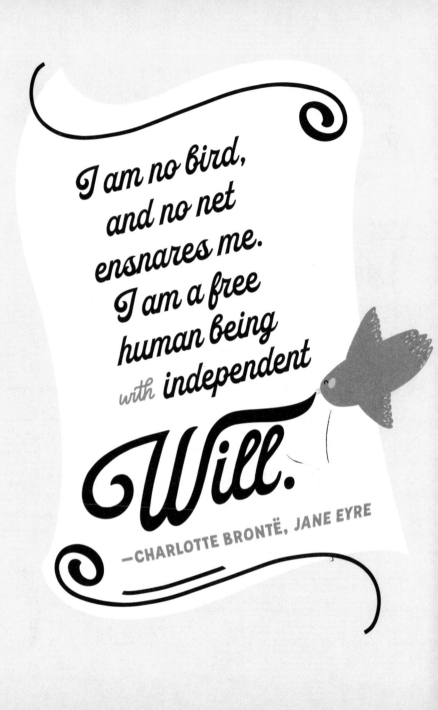

I am no bird,
and no net
ensnares me.
I am a free
human being
with independent

Will.

—CHARLOTTE BRONTË, JANE EYRE

Limitless

"I would, but..." is the death knell of manifestation. Make a list of the limitations or roadblocks you see in front of your goals. Next to them, write out how you could get around them or one reason why they might not be as bad as they seem.

Something unexpadable	Keep my focus in my Goal.
Having a bad day.	"
alcohol. drinken to much	"
no Money.	Find the way to find Money Make money.
My health.	Go to doctor.
other People Health.	Keep my focus in my God.
Noise	find a quiet place
Mess.	Clave. organize.
unltealthy environments.	leave or find a way.

Believe
IN YOURSELVES.
DREAM.
Try.
DO GOOD.
—MR. FEENY,
BOY MEETS WORLD

Simple Synchronicity

NOTES

Don't overcomplicate the message. Write down and repeat a few words that are meaningful to you: whether that means you feel them fully right now or you sure as fuck plan to feel them later.

You are Beatiful. Smart.

THERE ARE NO TRUE SOLO ACTS.
IF SOMEONE TELLS YOU THEY
GOT WHERE THEY ARE ALL BY
THEMSELVES, THEY'RE LYING.

—SAM DAVIDSON

A Lil Guiding Light

Good energy is not one-sided—it's a fucking prism. When have you felt another of those glimmering lights signaling the way? When has synchronicity found you or helpful energy been reflected back to you?

_____

_____

_____

_____

_____

_____

_____

_____

ISSA DEE: Do you listen to yourself?

KELLI PRENNY: All the time. I have a podcast.

—INSECURE

Broadcasting Live

Sure, not everything is going to be gold, but it's still worth its weight. What seemingly crazy shit have you said that inspired you or came true?

_____

_____

_____

_____

_____

_____

_____

_____

_____

_____

EVERY
ACTION
you → *take*
IS A VOTE FOR
THE TYPE OF PERSON
YOU WISH TO BECOME.

—JAMES CLEAR,
ATOMIC HABITS

Manifest Like You Mean It

Yes you can

never be afraid of change

What's waiting for you out there in the universe? Start with tiny, simple actions. Choose a morning mantra to say three times when you wake up. What is it? What's one step you can take beyond this nod to the universe that can help bring your goal to fruition?

_____

_____

_____

_____

_____

_____

_____

_____

I like it when
a flower or a
little tuft OF
grass grows
through a crack
in the concrete.
It's so fuckin' heroic.

—GEORGE CARLIN

Unlikely
Hero

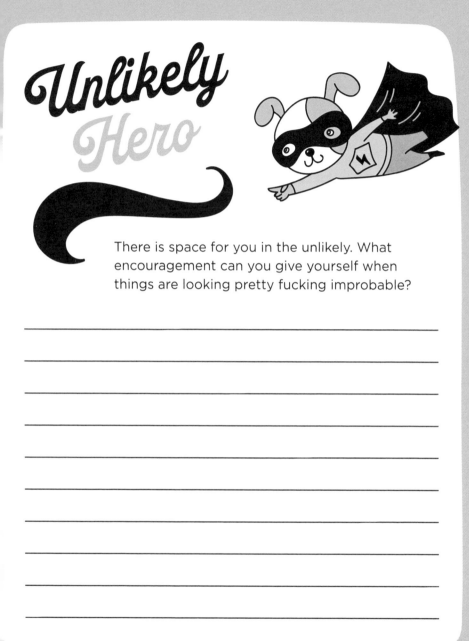

There is space for you in the unlikely. What encouragement can you give yourself when things are looking pretty fucking improbable?

_____

_____

_____

_____

_____

_____

_____

_____

_____

_____

It seems frankly **REMARKABLE** *that anyone anywhere* . . . EVER ATTEMPTED ANYTHING.

—DAVID RAKOFF,
SLATE

Visionary

Fire up that vision board! Whether the things you want for the future seem completely reasonable or batshit insane, you'd be surprised at the amazing things that come to pass. Write, draw, or paste the visions you have that are most important to you below.

NOTES

TODAY!

DO IT

I don't
BELIEVE in GUILTY PLEASURES;
I only believe in

PLEASURES.
PEOPLE WHO CALL READING
DETECTIVE FICTION OR
EATING DESSERT A
guilty pleasure
MAKE ME WANT TO PUKE.

—IRA GLASS

It's Been a Pleasure!

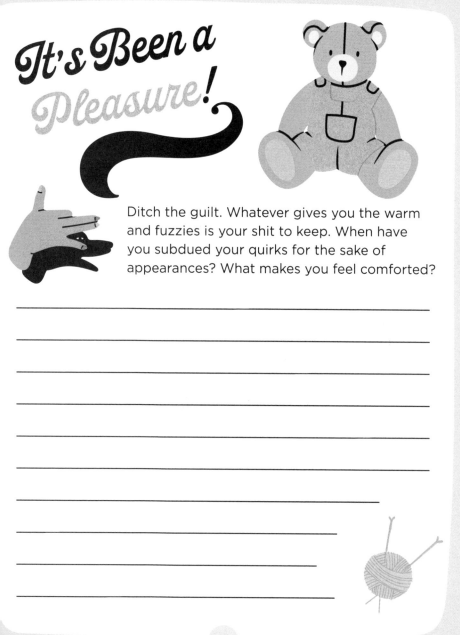

Ditch the guilt. Whatever gives you the warm and fuzzies is your shit to keep. When have you subdued your quirks for the sake of appearances? What makes you feel comforted?

_____

_____

_____

_____

_____

_____

_____

_____

_____

_____

Our

DEMONS LOSE THEIR POWER WHEN WE PULL THEM OUT *of the* **DEPTHS WHERE THEY HIDE** *and* **LOOK THEM** *in the* **FACE** *in* **BROAD DAYLIGHT.**

—ISABEL ALLENDE,
MAYA'S NOTEBOOK

Time to Vanquish!

It's hard to believe in your own power when there is a big, scary, what-the-fuck-is-that shadow in the background. But dispelling doubts makes the manifestation magic happen. What gets in the way of your ability to see and believe in your goals? Attack from a different angle. What weaknesses can you find in the things that are limiting you?

_____

_____

_____

_____

_____

_____

_____

_____

You may
THINK I'M SMALL,
but I have a
universe inside
my mind.

—YOKO ONO

Demand the Universe's Attention

WOOOO

Attracting attention to your manifestations might seem like a bit of a crapshoot. So give those symbolic statements flair: Write an intention to reject the things you don't need in your life on a piece of paper and let it burn. (Keep a fire extinguisher handy if you're prone to destruction!) Yell out your forward-momentum intentions to the sky so the universe can hear you better. What is it?

_____

_____

_____

_____

_____

_____

_____

_____

—ARIANA GRANDE,
JUST LIKE MAGIC

That's Attractive

Good energy attracts good energy. Choose a person who could use your love and light—whether this is a good friend or someone who needs to GTFO of your mind. Create a positive mantra to send their way and repeat it several times below.

_____

_____

_____

_____

_____

_____

_____

FAILURE IS AN ANSWER.

Rejection is an answer.

REGRET IS AN ETERNAL QUESTION

you will never have the answer to.

—TREVOR NOAH, *BORN A CRIME*

Letter from Your Future Badass

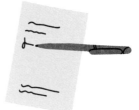

Write an entry from the perspective of your future self who has no regrets. What are you doing right now? Hold this person clearly in your mind as you visualize your future.

_____

_____

_____

_____

_____

_____

_____

_____

_____

_____

_____

I DON'T HAVE

TIME

TO **SUFFER.**

THINKING ABOUT HOW I'M LESS THAN DOESN'T MAKE ME FEEL GOOD.

—DAX SHEPHERD, *ARMCHAIR EXPERT*

Tick Tock!

Time's a-wasting. Set your timer for 30 seconds. Write out all of the ways you currently feel or want to feel "more than" without stopping.

_____

_____

_____

_____

_____

_____

_____

_____

_____

_____

_____

_____

THOSE ARE OUR PROVERBIAL ONIONS, RAW AND PEELED. AND YOURS?

Care to peel for us.?

—OLIVER PUTNAM,
ONLY MURDERS IN THE BUILDING

Everyone is Crying

Some people are better at being vulnerable than others. It stings, and then suddenly your eyes are leaking and you don't know what to do with all that extra moisture. Weird! But it's time to peel some onions because it's good for everyone involved. What makes you feel vulnerable? What could you make with those vulnerable parts of you?

_____

_____

_____

_____

_____

_____

_____

_____

I HAVE TRIED HARD — BUT

Life

IS DIFFICULT, AND I AM A VERY USELESS PERSON.

—EDITH WHARTON,
HOUSE OF MIRTH

Pardon Me While I Emotionally Flail

It can feel like all you do is work and sweat while you're in weeds, yet those roses just refuse to come the fuck up. When you've hit your limit, let yourself do some proper kicking and screaming. What kind of catharsis (that doesn't ruin someone else's day!) do you need?

_____

_____

_____

_____

_____

_____

_____

_____

*What are
you going to do?*
EVERYTHING, IS MY
GUESS. IT WILL BE A
LITTLE MESSY, BUT

embrace the mess.

 IT WILL BE
COMPLICATED,
*but rejoice in the
complications.*

—NORA EPHRON

Take the Scenic Route

WHOOPSIES!

Manifestation is not linear. It has detours, it has bumps, and it has the occasional clusterfuck—but it can also surprise you. The beauty of having an open heart for what's to come is that the mess can take you places you didn't know you could go. What expectations do you have about the road ahead? What can you say to yourself if it goes differently than planned?

_____

_____

_____

_____

_____

_____

_____

_____

Make FINE DREAMS

—TOM ROBBINS,
FIERCE INVALIDS HOME
FROM HOT CLIMATES

Is this real life?

Dreams are what you make them. Scribble, doodle, or write out a dream that feels so real it could jump right off the fucking page. What about this dream do you know to be true?

_____

_____

_____

_____

_____

_____

_____

_____

_____

_____

Really,

HOW IS
EATING
A PIECE
of *Cake*

BAD? BEING BAD IS MURDERING SOMEONE. THAT'S BAD. *Don't do that.*

—SARAH MICHELLE GELLAR

Relatively Speaking

Let's agree that torture is a no-no. Yes? Cool. This includes torturing yourself. Whether you're on a health, financial, or personal journey—try not to attach guilt to goals. When have you broken one of your own rules and found that lightning didn't strike you dead? What reminders can you give yourself that indulgences are okay?

_____

_____

_____

_____

_____

_____

_____

YOU HAVE BEEN
CRITIZING YOURSELF
FOR YEARS, AND IT
HASN'T WORKED.
TRY APPROVING OF

Yourself
AND

SEE WHAT HAPPENS.

—LOUISE L. HAY

You're Doing So Well!

Fuck the criticism. Choose one way to approve of yourself—whether it comes easily or not—and repeat it below.

_____

_____

_____

_____

_____

_____

_____

_____

_____

_____

$\mathcal{A}+$

If a crystal ball fell in my lap, I WOULD STILL GAZE INTO IT. I WOULD LISTEN TO WHAT IT HAD TO SAY. BUT NOW I TAKE EVERYTHING PEOPLE TELL ME WITH A GRAIN OF SALT. *I no longer feel as if there were anyone who knows more than I do.*

**—SELMA BLAIR,
MEAN BABY**

Be Your Own Crystal Ball

8

What you feel in your gut matters. When has someone directed you away from something you knew was right for you? What can you say to yourself to prove that you know the way?

_____

_____

_____

_____

_____

_____

_____

_____

_____

_____

ONCE I STOP
PEOPLE-PLEASING

IT'S OVER FOR

👍 YOU 👍

BITCHES

IF THAT'S OK *with* YOU,
NO WORRIES IF NOT!

—LANE MOORE

Bitch, Please

What kind of sassy strength do you want to feel on a regular basis? Whether it's taking a deep breath or humming three seconds of your favorite anthem, how could you pause and regroup before you jump to people-pleasing?

You gotta COME TO terms with THE LOW POINTS

—HASSAN MINAJ,
THE ROOMMATES
PODCAST

Peace Offering

Manifesting good energy and positive results doesn't mean that low points will never happen. In case they do, have something in your back pocket to get you back on track. What bit of comfort or encouragement—whether it's a lyric, or a memory, or a peppy reminder that you are a fucking badass—helps bring you peace?

_____

_____

_____

_____

_____

_____

_____

_____

_____

I'm not going TO downplay

MY STRENGTHS
SO YOU FEEL
LESS SHITTY
ABOUT YOUR OWN
SHORTCOMINGS.

—ILIZA SHLESINGER,
GIRL LOGIC

Shine Bright, Bitch :)

Don't let other people's insecurities dim your sparkle. What are your strengths? How will these strengths bring you closer to your goals?

_____

_____

_____

_____

_____

_____

_____

_____

_____

_____

HOW DO YOU KNOW WHAT IS
the right path
TO CHOOSE TO GET THE
RESULT THAT YOU DESIRE?
THE HONEST ANSWER IS THIS:
You won't.
AND ACCEPTING
THAT GREATLY EASES THE
ANXIETY OF YOUR
LIFE EXPERIENCE.

—JON STEWART

Destiny, Next Left

It's okay not to know how you're going to get somewhere. Visualize your ideal scenario five years from now. Where are you? What does the space look like? How does your heart feel?

_____

_____

_____

_____

_____

_____

_____

_____

_____

It's **IMPOSSIBLE** TO BE

PERFECT,

and you won't do a good job if you're too focused on proving yourself to others.

—JESSICA WILLIAMS

Perfect Pretty Fucking Great!

Peach & Peace
the
SWEET SCENT
of MIND YOUR
OWN BEESWAX

THIS IS *my diary*
WRITTEN BY
MY DAMN SELF

Keep other people out of your manifestations if they don't belong in the mix. In what ways can you give yourself some slack? How can you focus on what you want for yourself instead of what others think?

REAL GENEROSITY IS ALSO SHOWING UP WHEN YOU DON'T FEEL LIKE IT —

SACRIFICING

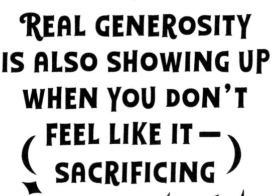

your

own

HAPPINESS IN EXCHANGE FOR SOMEONE ELSE'S.

—CHELSEA HANDLER,
LIFE WILL BE THE DEATH OF ME

Fork It Over

Be generous with your time and space. (Not to be confused with being a lovely but much-used doormat.) How is caring about others—and showing them, too!—meaningful and part of your journey? When has someone done this for you?

_____

_____

_____

_____

_____

_____

_____

_____

I was born as sweet as that and if I am too sweet FOR your tastes then

JUST CLAMP YOUR MOUTH SHUT AND SPIN ON YOUR HEELS.

—JENNY SLATE,
LITTLE WEIRDS

Fucking *Sweet!*

Reject the idea that you have to change your ingredients to be the right flavor for someone else. When has being yourself worked out in your favor? What about being true to yourself can attract everything you need?

_____

_____

_____

_____

_____

_____

_____

_____

I THINK

you

HAVE TO HAVE FAITH IN PEOPLE BEFORE THEY EARN IT. OTHERWISE IT'S NOT FAITH, RIGHT?

—TAYLOR JENKINS REID,
DAISY JONES & THE SIX

Yes Way!

♥ TRUST THE PROCESS

You can either start a journey with "there's no way that can happen" or be delightfully astounded and shout "no fucking way!" when it actually does. What feels good about trusting the process and the people around you? What kind of momentum can this energy create?

_____

_____

_____

_____

_____

_____

_____

_____

When in doubt,
MAKE
FUNNY FACES.

—AMY POEHLER

Just for Funsies

Take a step back from the serious shit. When could loosening your expectations and opening yourself up to more fun feel better? What about that attitude could attract more fun energy more often?

_____

_____

_____

_____

_____

_____

_____

_____

_____

_____

I'm the worst night owl,

BECAUSE I'M

a self-loathing night owl

WHO THINKS,

No, I should be getting up early.

—RONNY CHIENG

Be Yourself for Fuck's Sake

Square peg, round hole and all that! Identify the needs that you may be trying to squash because you have a preconceived notion that they're bad. Why are you trying to fix them? How could making some adjustments allow you to meet these needs instead of compromising them?

_____

_____

_____

_____

_____

_____

_____

_____

_____

_____

GOOD THINGS, *you can't* RUSH INTO THEM.

—JOSÉ ANDRES

It's On the Way

The End

Patience sounds really cute until you actually have to have it. When you're itching for something to come to you, there's a constant reel playing in the background telling you what you lack. What relief could you feel if you trust that good things will come? What could this knowledge do if it's what's playing in the background?

_____

_____

_____

_____

_____

_____

_____

_____

NO RESERVATIONS, NO EDITS.

Nasty shit!

...I FIND INSPIRATION IN MOMENTS THAT CHALLENGE OUR IDEAS ON WHAT IT MEANS TO BE

loved

OR ACCEPTED.

—BENITO SKINNER, *THE CUT*

Get Real

What unfiltered advice or encouragement have you found most inspiring? When has someone changed your perspective by shaking things up?

_____

_____

_____

_____

_____

_____

_____

_____

_____

_____

_____

It's weird, huh?

IT'S LIKE THE
MINUTE YOU
KINDA GIVE UP
CONTROL YOU
JUST KNOW WHAT
TO DO WITHOUT
DOING ANYTHING.

—AUBREY PLAZA

Fuck the "How"

Sometimes when you stop exhaustively trying to map out every inch of the process, things seem to magically align. Worry less about the "how" of what you want and project the energy that it will be. Write a thank you note to yourself or to someone important as if what you're looking for has already happened. What does it say?

_____

_____

_____

_____

_____

_____

_____

_____

Work hard, KNOW YOUR SHIT, show your shit, AND THEN FEEL ENTITLED.

—MINDY KALING, WHY NOT ME?

Nailed It!

When has working hard for something and succeeding made you feel fucking phenomenal?

_____

_____

_____

_____

_____

_____

_____

_____

_____

_____

_____

You draw **YOUR** own box.

YOU INTRODUCE YOURSELF AS WHO YOU ARE. . . YOU CREATE THE IDENTITY YOU WANT FOR YOURSELF.

—MEGHAN MARKLE

Line It Up

Align yourself with what you want to be in the world. Who or what makes you feel like you are ever closer to your aspirations?

_____

_____

_____

_____

_____

_____

_____

_____

_____

_____

I'm not going to die because **I FAILED** *as someone else. I'm going* TO **SUCCEED** *as myself.*

—MARGARET CHO

Fuck Yes, Success!

FINISH

When has trying to be more like someone else failed you? When has staying in your lane let you speed on ahead?

_____

_____

_____

_____

_____

_____

_____

_____

_____

MY ANSWER WHENEVER I
AM ASKED ABOUT IMPOSTER
SYNDROME IS TO ADMIT THAT

I am an imposter,

AND I TREAT IT LIKE CRASHING
A WEDDING. YOU'RE IN NOW, HAVE

as much fun as possible

AND GRAB ALL THE CAKE YOU CAN
BEFORE SOMEONE THROWS YOU OUT.

Lean in and make it a party.

—JAMEELA JAMIL

Party On!

Feeling like an imposter? Welcome to the costume party called Life. Dress up and celebrate like you know what the fuck you are doing and enjoy! In what situation can you try out your new 'fit?

_____

_____

_____

_____

_____

_____

_____

_____

_____

_____

THE BEST THING YOU CAN POSSIBLY DO WITH YOUR *Life*

IS TO TACKLE THE MOTHERFUCKING SHIT OUT OF IT.

—CHERYL STRAYED,
TINY BEAUTIFUL THINGS

Get a Life!

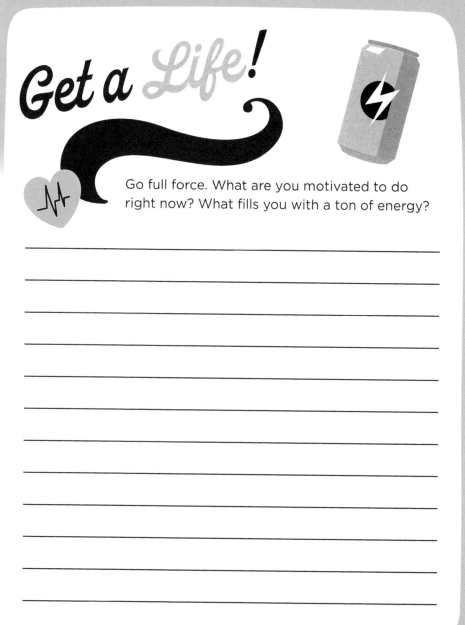

Go full force. What are you motivated to do right now? What fills you with a ton of energy?

_____

_____

_____

_____

_____

_____

_____

_____

_____

_____

_____

_____

_____

DON'T

Dream IT.

BE IT.

—TIM CURRY,
*THE ROCKY HORROR
PICTURE SHOW*